No Secrets to Elevation

CALVIN MILLS, JR.

The
Great Idea
Journal

A 12-MONTH GUIDE
TO ENTREPRENEURIAL
PERSISTENCE

This Journal Belongs to

_____

_____

NO SECRETS TO ELEVATION | **THE GREAT IDEA JOURNAL**:
A 12-MONTH GUIDE TO ENTREPRENEURIAL PERSISTENCE

Copyright © 2018 Calvin Mills, Jr.

All rights reserved.

ISBN-13: 978-1722041601
ISBN-10: 1722041609

Start your journey to success with 12 months of persistence.

HOW DO YOU USE THIS JOURNAL?

First, get that great idea of yours down on paper! Write it out on the next page. Second, start building a list of books you'll want to read over the next 12 months. From there, each month you will learn a new focus point, answer insightful questions and record your thoughts, business plans or meeting notes. By the end of the 12-month period, you will have brought your great idea to life and set your career on a path to long-term success.

WHAT'S THE FOCUS INSIDE?

- ➤ **MONTH 1:** Cultivating Your Idea in Your Market
- ➤ **MONTH 2:** The Truth About Entrepreneurship
- ➤ **MONTH 3:** Sacrifice
- ➤ **MONTH 4:** Planning & Setting Goals
- ➤ **MONTH 5:** Preparing for Growth
- ➤ **MONTH 6:** Beyond the Textbook
- ➤ **MONTH 7:** Self-Care
- ➤ **MONTH 8:** Defining Success
- ➤ **MONTH 9:** Facing Your Fears
- ➤ **MONTH 10:** Ensuring Stability
- ➤ **MONTH 11:** Turning Impossible into *I'm Possible*
- ➤ **MONTH 12:** Leadership
- ➤ **REFLECTIVE QUESTIONS**

MY READING LIST

Build a list of books you're reading or plan
to read within the next 12 months.

_____

_____

_____

_____

_____

_____

_____

_____

_____

_____

_____

_____

_____

_____

_____

_____

_____

WHAT IS YOUR GREAT IDEA?

_____

_____

_____

_____

_____

_____

_____

_____

_____

_____

_____

_____

_____

_____

_____

_____

FOCUS:

Cultivating Your Idea
in Your Market

*Your customers will always tell you what
direction you should go in.*

What's a great idea without a plan and market to succeed in?

While it is easy to get caught up in the excitement of launching a new product or starting your own business, don't overlook the importance of conducting proper research specific to your market. Sadly, so many great ideas fail in producing a sales profit by ignoring the answer to this key element: *How to win over new customers?* When you don't have new customers rolling in, it means you won't gain sales. No sales mean no profit, and no profit guarantees no success.

Early on, research your market and discover the unmet needs of your target customers. Study the details of your demographic (including their age, gender, popular occupational choices, hobbies, etc.) and explore the complications that accompany their daily lives. Put yourself in their shoes to determine whether or not your service(s) will fill their voids and generate enough motive to result in a purchase.

Customers are constantly reminded by personal difficulties and are actively looking for solutions. Knowing your future audience and understanding how your great idea meets their demands will make positioning your product easier and more accurate.

Is there a market for your idea? If so, describe it.

_____

_____

_____

_____

What companies are already in that market?

_____

_____

_____

How can you be competitive in this market?

_____

_____

_____

What niche is the market missing? How can your
idea fill this niche?

_____

_____

_____

_____

_____

WEEK 1

WEEK 2

WEEK 3

WEEK 4

FOCUS:

The Truth About Entrepreneurship

... it takes a special person to step out and say, "I have no clue when I am going to get paid, but I know what I can control.

If you're still working a 9-5 job, face unhappiness and disappointment by preparing an exit plan — a plan for how you will walk away from the situation.

Being an entrepreneur is like constantly being on a battlefield, fighting for and against yourself.

You're constantly doubting yourself, wondering if what you're doing is good enough to make an impact. The truth is, being an entrepreneur is a challenge, but through determination and a clear reason on starting a business, you will soar above the obstacles.

The entrepreneur-life comes with sacrifice and risk. By beginning a business, you vow to sacrifice your money, your mind, and your leisure for a dream you've finally had the courage to display. But with this sacrifice comes doubt: Have you made the right decision? Will this be worth it? What if you fail? To become a strong entrepreneur, you have to push through those fears, turn a blind eye to the doubts, and marvel in what's to come. The rewards will make the sacrifice worth it.

Push yourself to take risks and remain optimistic while doing so. Don't let the stress weigh you down, and don't let those doubts muddle your ultimate goal. Allow yourself to be humble, to take criticism and learn from it. Then, stand firm and fight hard for your business because the real truth about being an entrepreneur is that only you can make you dream into a reality.

Instead of listing everything you have at risk, list everything that motivates you to keep going.

_____

_____

_____

_____

_____

_____

_____

What doubts are keeping you from taking your entrepreneurship to the next level? How can you combat it?

_____

_____

_____

_____

_____

Through your challenges, how can you transfer something you've learned into a pillar for your success?

_____

_____

_____

_____

_____

WEEK 1

WEEK 2

WEEK 3

WEEK 4

**3rd
Month**_____

FOCUS:

Sacrifice

*If you want to become successful or
legendary, first understand what it means to
make some sacrifices.*

The benefits that come with the exciting lifestyle of entrepreneurship aren't without sacrifice.

At any time, especially in the early developing stages, your business plan could be in jeopardy. Are you willing to make the sacrifices required to continue on your path to success?

You will be forced to make critical choices that could affect both your business and personal life. You'll find yourself deciding between this and that on many occasions. Like giving up a stable paycheck for what could be a few rocky months ahead. Missing out on quality time spent with family and friends. Spending less time doing the things you used to love. At times you may even lose your own sanity.

Prepare yourself for these difficulties by knowing exactly what lengths you are willing to go to keep your great idea alive and in motion. Keep in mind, the more you are willing to give now, the more you will receive in the future.

What are you willing to sacrifice mentally and emotionally?

_____

_____

_____

_____

What are you willing to sacrifice financially?

_____

_____

_____

_____

What are you willing to sacrifice physically?

_____

_____

_____

_____

Who will you turn to for support with these sacrifices?

_____

_____

_____

_____

_____

WEEK 1

WEEK 2

WEEK 3

WEEK 4

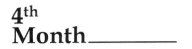

FOCUS:

Planning & Setting Goals

Preparation-focus-determination" — If you're not focused on what you want and determined to make it happen, it doesn't matter how great your idea is on paper or in your mind. It'll never come to life.

In order for your great idea to reach its full potential, you must consistently strive to do more.

Never settle on where you're at in your business plan when there is always room for growth. Goal setting is a great way to stay motivated and progressively move forward. Without goals, you may find yourself lost in the progress and lose sight of the big picture.

When planning your goals remember to keep them simple and measurable. Simplicity cuts down on future confusion while measurable data provides tangible evidence. The information you gather from goal setting should highlight both your developing strengths and weaknesses. Record these changes on annual and quarterly reports; this will provide visual representation on your progress. A successful business will be an ever-changing one so it's important that your goals adjust to your current situation.

Achieving a goal no matter how simple calls for celebration. Reward yourself and your supporting team on a job well done.

Are your goals measurable? How so?

_____

_____

_____

_____

What are your one-year goals?

_____

_____

_____

_____

What are your five-year goals?

_____

_____

_____

_____

What are your ten-year or longer goals?

_____

_____

_____

_____

_____

WEEK 1

WEEK 2

WEEK 3

WEEK 4

FOCUS:

Preparing for Growth

We want to live out our dreams, not our duties. We want a long-term plan that still includes endless, unexpected opportunities.

Growth spurts happen. Sometimes they are fast, sometimes slow.

Sometimes a lot changes, sometimes not much at all. But growth happens and one might struggle to adjust. How are you preparing for the possibility of any growth type? Fast or slow? Big changes or little changes? As you learned last month, leadership is about courage and confidence; to sustain growth and prepare for growth (or decline), one must have the courage to plan for any path the business walks down.

It's important to be open-minded when it comes to growth. It won't happen exactly as you plan it. Therefore, any leader must consider every avenue that can be walked down — whether it's sustainable growth, volatile growth, or decline — and create a procedure that the business will be able to follow once that path is starting to take shape. This plan is not a blueprint nor a set-in-stone endeavor; rather, this plan is to nudge you into the right direction and keep you focused. If the growth is more than you can handle, it is important to keep your eyes clear and weather the storm. Don't let the rain wash you away.

Another important aspect of growth is tracking it. What methodologies are you using to gauge your level of growth? How much growth would you like to have in the first year? The first five? What happens when that growth starts to plateau? To nosedive? Tracking growth is tracking hope — it's not a science, but it is a guideline to keep you sane. The business will not be where it was when it started; your job is to grow it to where you want it, and keeping track of that growth is how you will get to where you want to be.

If your business grows rapidly upon launching, what steps would you take to ensure that you are able to manage the changes?

_____

_____

_____

_____

What will be your methods for tracking growth?

_____

_____

_____

What contingencies do you have in place for potential decline?

_____

_____

_____

What do the growth patterns look like in the other companies in your field? What can you learn from them for your own endeavors?

_____

_____

_____

_____

_____

WEEK 1

WEEK 2

WEEK 3

WEEK 4

FOCUS:

Beyond the Textbook

*Schools aren't internally structured to teach
us how to be entrepreneurs. They teach us
how to get a good education, a secure job
and then retire.*

*It's not all about the level of education
you've achieved.*

You can learn the basic knowledge on how to run a successful business by investing tens of thousands of dollars on a college education.

The years spent listening to lectures on sales tactics, marketing strategies and financial options will prove to be beneficial in the startup of your company. However, it is only a matter of time before you realize real life experience, an essential component to business, can't be found in a textbook.

Seek opportunities that will allow you to gain hands on experiences to running a business. Learn the secrets to success and the hidden messages only current business owners can share. Write down different methods that work and what doesn't; ideas that you like and dislike. Ask questions that none of your professors were able to answer. Take advantage and get a head start in your own business planning.

Keep in mind, what works for one business may not work for yours. Learn as much as you can, but uniqueness in your own ideas is what makes one successful.

**What are some things you wished college
better prepared you for?**

_____

_____

_____

_____

**How does your great idea differ from what you
learned in college?**

_____

_____

_____

_____

**What real life experiences can provide you with great
learning opportunities?**

_____

_____

_____

_____

**What would you like to learn by working with other
entrepreneurs in your field?**

_____

_____

_____

_____

_____

WEEK 1

WEEK 2

WEEK 3

WEEK 4

FOCUS:

Self-Care

The question is not, "What does it cost?"
The question is how much are you willing to
invest mentally, emotionally and physically
to turn your vision into reality?

It goes without saying that being an entrepreneur is hard work.

It costs not only your mental health, but your physical and emotional health as well. Between the stressors of decision-making, the balance between your work and personal life, and your own personal health, it is important to find stability and avoid burning out through overworking.

This month, find a support group. This can be anyone — friends, family, or coworkers and employees — but no matter who they are, allow them to support you in your endeavors and keep you optimistic when you feel defeated.

Breathe, relax, and set boundaries. Give yourself a break because you deserve it. And during that break, do what you enjoy outside of work. Whether this is reading, watching movies, or gardening, allot yourself enough time to enjoy life and get away from any stressful demands or tasks.

Balance is the key to becoming a strong and healthy entrepreneur. Always remember to first take care of yourself. Give yourself enough time to revel in the magnificence of life. Then, remind yourself of why you chose the entrepreneur-life in the first place. Use that motivation to balance yourself and become a leader in your field.

As an entrepreneur and leader in your field, how do you expect to handle the stressors of managing your own venture?

_____

_____

_____

_____

In what ways can you establish balance between work and relaxation?

_____

_____

_____

_____

How can you take care of those who work for you or assist in the development?

_____

_____

_____

_____

Write a daily regimen that promotes self-care.

_____

_____

_____

_____

_____

_____

WEEK 1

WEEK 2

WEEK 3

WEEK 4

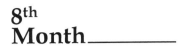
FOCUS:

Defining Success

*Strength — It means to remain fixed on the
dream, in character, condition and position,
regardless of anything trying to pull you
away from it.*

Success is the feeling you get when you accomplish a goal.

Success is the growth you see in not only you but your employees and company. Success is the long-term goal for any entrepreneur. It's more than money and power. It's achievements and change. Success is what makes you a defining entrepreneur.

Forget about the paths other successful entrepreneurs have taken: pave your own. Set yourself some short-term goals, stepping stones to the ultimate goal of success. By creating short-term goals and achieving them, you are molding your career around the original purpose you began this journey, and you are allowing yourself and your company to grow. Excellence takes time; let it ripen before you pick it.

Continuously surprise yourself and those around you with the amount of courage and strength you have to dive into the business world head-on. Always have an optimistic smile, and don't let failure ruin you. Use it to your advantage and motivate yourself to try new strategies and listen to and learn from criticism. Give yourself enough time to grow and learn, and never lose your confidence because the path you are paving will eventually lead to success.

Who do you define as successful entrepreneur(s)?

_____

_____

_____

_____

What do you believe makes the people you
listed successful?

_____

_____

_____

_____

List short-term goals you have as an entrepreneur.

_____

_____

_____

_____

How do you plan to accomplish your goals?

_____

_____

_____

_____

_____

_____

WEEK 1

WEEK 2

WEEK 3

WEEK 4

FOCUS:

Facing Your Fears

*Challenges are what make life interesting
and overcoming them is what makes life
meaningful. Never fear failing at something
because there's something you have to learn.*

*When you truly believe in your vision, you'll
act in a way that supports it for the long
haul.*

Although not a favorable subject, failure is inevitable for all entrepreneurs.

As human beings we hate to fail and the fear of failure can drive one to make poor decisions in order to avoid potential damages to one's image. Instead of choosing to accept failure, develop a new mindset of failing forward. With a forward-thinking attitude you can still defy the odds and continue on the path to success.

Think of your failures as simple setbacks. Setbacks are no reason to completely uproot your entire business plan or give up entirely. You will however want to go back and discover where in your business plan weaknesses overpowered your strengths. From there you can move forward and start fresh writing up new objectives. Avoid additional stress by keeping your focus on the things you can control.

Failure in a business doesn't mean a failed business. With a new flexible way of thinking and a willingness to change; you can take back the power in your idea. Believing in your own worth will make it that much easier for others to see it as well.

Document your failures so you may learn from them. What are a few you can think of that you've learned from thus far?

_____

_____

_____

_____

What are your strengths? What are your weaknesses?

_____

_____

_____

_____

No idea is a complete failure. What are the pinpoints in your business plan that have been less successful?

_____

_____

_____

_____

Go back to brainstorming. What ideas can you rule out? How will you replace them?

_____

_____

_____

_____

_____

WEEK 1

WEEK 2

WEEK 3

WEEK 4

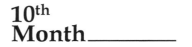

FOCUS:

Ensuring Stability

*The more you practice and build a certain
characteristic, you can always become what
you may not be at this very moment.*

Being an entrepreneur is very different from providing a good, stable product to the masses. Everyone wants success, but here's what sets you apart — endurance. If you can offer endurance and stability in an ever-changing world with new products, trends, and choices, the probability of your business succeeding grows exponentially.

Architects build houses and bridges for the long-term. They don't rush; they plan. They make solid structures that are built to last. Your company must do the same. To create a successful enterprise, you must look at every aspect of your product—strengths and weaknesses — and develop safeguards to protect from volatility. What works well? Make sure it stays well. What doesn't work well? Make sure it's fixed before it's too late. No architect wants to know their bridge collapsed; they plan years ahead to make sure it will still provide its service even a decade in advance. Your business must prolong that longevity in much the same manner.

Find what makes your business unique and hone it. Stabilize it. Streamline it. Never stop perfecting it. If you do, someone else might swoop in and steal your market. In fact, you should plan for someone to come in and steal your market; how would you respond? Is your product good enough to outlast that challenge? No one has a crystal ball that they can look through to see what their future holds but everyone has the next best thing: the ability to prepare. Ensure stability by ensuring your plans are correct and the future is as wide open for you and your business as possible.

List qualities of your product/service that prove
that it is enduring.

_____

_____

_____

_____

Which of the qualities you listed can be further
improved?

_____

_____

_____

Where can you implement longevity strategies? Are
there any obvious holes that need filling in?

_____

_____

_____

As it's often said, "It takes a village." Who can you
recruit at this stage to help stabilize your vision?

_____

_____

_____

_____

_____

_____

WEEK 1

WEEK 2

WEEK 3

WEEK 4

FOCUS:

Turning Impossible into *I'm Possible*

Always believe in yourself. The minute you give up on yourself, you give up on everything you are.

... look at the word 'impossible' and see 'I'm possible' every time.

Nothing is impossible.

You've heard that phrase a million times, it's an echo in your mind. The entrepreneurial lifestyle is filled with obstacles, some of which stop you dead in your tracks. Do you really want to take that risk? Should you turn around? Can this even be done? Clear your mind of those pesky thoughts of impossibility. Don't let them hinder the journey of your entrepreneurship.

To prosper in an entrepreneur's world, you must learn the language of achievement and possibility and whole-heartedly believe it. Think outside the box and step out of your comfort zone because in order to flourish in the business world, you must free yourself of the ordinary and fill yourself with the big dreams you've developed over the course of your journey. Think "I can" to challenges you would normally avoid and those yet to come, and remove "impossible" from your vocabulary entirely.

Lastly, identify the challenges that are blocking your path, and recognize the "why." Why are they challenges, and why can't you get past them? Seeing them as simple words on paper makes them smaller and clearer, thus making them easier to accomplish. Don't let your career as an entrepreneur overpower your positivity. Replace "impossible" with "I'm Possible" and face your challenges head on.

Nearing the end of your first year developing your great idea, what challenges are intimidating you?

_____

_____

_____

_____

What makes something "impossible"
in the first place?

_____

_____

_____

How do you plan to face your challenges from
this point forward?

_____

_____

_____

_____

_____

_____

_____

_____

_____

_____

WEEK 1

WEEK 2

WEEK 3

WEEK 4

FOCUS:

Leadership

Even as a leader, you'll find others you can learn from. The cycle of following and leading (learning and teaching) never stops.

Before one can lead, one must first follow.

Leadership is one of the most important qualities to running a successful business but no successful businessman has begun from thin air; the vision and direction it takes to lead comes from past leaders you have admired (or despised) while gaining knowledge and education. Ask yourself: whose leadership am I modeling my leadership after? Whose leadership do I not want to emulate? Who dictated tasks effectively? Who did not? By asking these sorts of questions, one will learn what qualities they admired in their past bosses and learn to apply them once they themselves take the reigns.

Having understood which qualities you wish to imitate, it is important you know how to effectively execute those qualities as a leader. It is one thing to admire a past boss' handling of a specific situation but it is another entity entirely when faced with a similar problem that you must now face. Leadership takes guts, courage, and wherewithal. Putting leadership qualities into action takes audacity. You will have to make tough decisions; you will have to stand by those tough decisions. Like leaders before you, it is important you understand that to lead is to move forward; retreating from responsibilities ruins the business' opportunity for growth. Confidence in leadership is the only path where your business will find a way into the future.

List the names of leaders you admire.

_____

_____

_____

_____

How can you apply those qualities seen in others
to better your own leadership style?

_____

_____

_____

_____

Are you willing to lead others? If so, how?

_____

_____

_____

_____

Where are you leading others? How far are you
willing to take them?

_____

_____

_____

_____

_____

WEEK 1

WEEK 2

WEEK 3

WEEK 4

Once you believe in yourself, identify your gifts and find the purpose of those gifts, there will be no limit to what you are capable of achieving.

REFLECTIVE QUESTIONS

What habits helped successfully develop the first stages of your great idea?

_____

_____

_____

_____

_____

_____

_____

_____

How have you learned from failure?

_____

_____

_____

_____

_____

_____

_____

How did you make your first sale?

_____

_____

_____

_____

_____

_____

_____

_____

How did you develop key partnerships?

_____

_____

_____

_____

_____

_____

_____

_____

_____

How did you distinguish yourself from your competitors?

_____

_____

_____

_____

_____

_____

_____

_____

What was your biggest mistake?

_____

_____

_____

_____

_____

_____

_____

_____

If you go back to earlier months in the process,
what would you have done differently?

_____

_____

_____

_____

_____

_____

_____

_____

How do you keep your focus on the big picture in
the midst of many small responsibilities?

_____

_____

_____

_____

_____

_____

_____

_____

What's your best advice for someone who has an
idea but doesn't know where to start?

_____

_____

_____

_____

_____

_____

_____

_____

_____

**SHARE YOUR REFLECTIVE ANSWERS
WITH A FRIEND.**

ABOUT THE AUTHOR

Calvin Mills Jr. is an award-winning serial entrepreneur, dynamic speaker, mentor and the author of *No Secrets to Elevation: An Entrepreneur's Story of Persistence*. He built his nationally recognized platform in the information technology arena from humble beginnings. Succeeding as the Founder, CEO and President of CMC Technology Solutions, Calvin has been featured in Entrepreneur, Fast Company, and InfoWorld publications.

From the start of his career, he has focused his pursuit on making a people-focused mark in his industry, and today, he continues to make a great difference in the lives of the next generation of entrepreneurs. He and his wife and children live in Baton Rouge, Louisiana.

Made in the USA
Columbia, SC
01 August 2023

21033010R00100